YELLOWSTONE
National Park

BY CHRIS BOWMAN

BELLWETHER MEDIA • MINNEAPOLIS, MN

Blastoff! Discovery launches a new mission: reading to learn. Filled with facts and features, each book offers you an exciting new world to explore!

BLASTOFF! UNIVERSE

BLASTOFF! Beginners
GRADE K

BLASTOFF! READERS
GRADES 1-3

BLASTOFF! DISCOVERY
GRADE 4

This edition first published in 2023 by Bellwether Media, Inc.

No part of this publication may be reproduced in whole or in part without written permission of the publisher.
For information regarding permission, write to Bellwether Media, Inc.,
Attention: Permissions Department,
6012 Blue Circle Drive, Minnetonka, MN 55343.

Library of Congress Cataloging-in-Publication Data

Names: Bowman, Chris, 1990- author.
Title: Yellowstone National Park / by Chris Bowman.
Description: Minneapolis, MN : Bellwether Media, Inc., 2023. |
   Series: Blastoff! Discovery : U.S. national parks | Includes bibliographical
   references and index. | Audience: Ages 7-13 | Audience: Grades 4-6 |
   Summary: "Engaging images accompany information about Yellowstone
   National Park. The combination of high-interest subject matter and narrative
   text is intended for students in grades 3 through 8"– Provided by publisher.
Identifiers: LCCN 2022016504 (print) | LCCN 2022016505 (ebook) |
   ISBN 9781644877562 (library binding) | ISBN 9781648348020 (ebook)
Subjects: LCSH: Yellowstone National Park–Juvenile literature.
Classification: LCC F722 .B69 2023 (print) | LCC F722 (ebook) |
   DDC 978.7/52–dc23/eng/20220414
LC record available at https://lccn.loc.gov/2022016504
LC ebook record available at https://lccn.loc.gov/2022016505

Editor: Betsy Rathburn
Series Design: Jeffrey Kollock   Book Designer: Laura Sowers

Printed in the United States of America, North Mankato, MN.

TABLE OF CONTENTS

A DAY IN YELLOWSTONE

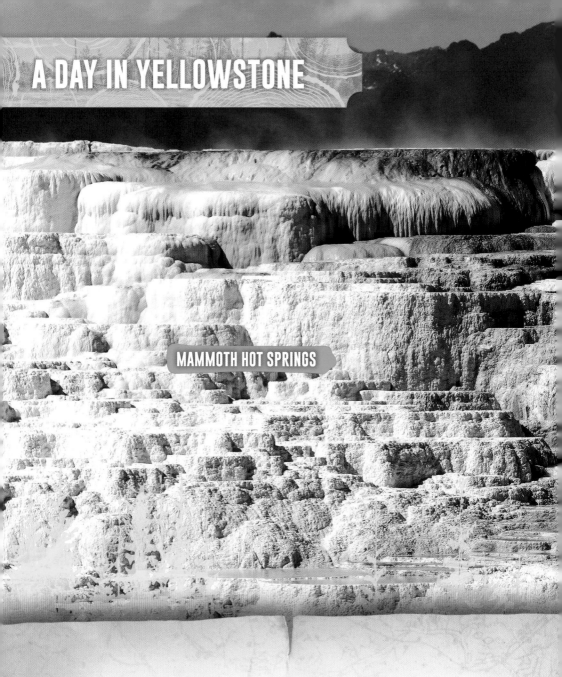

MAMMOTH HOT SPRINGS

A family drives into Yellowstone National Park. They have an exciting day planned. Their first stop is Mammoth **Hot Springs**. They are amazed by the steaming white and orange **terraces**!

GRAND CANYON OF THE
YELLOWSTONE RIVER

The family then drives to Artist Point. From here, they have a great view of a waterfall in the Grand Canyon of the Yellowstone River. Finally, the family heads to nearby Hayden Valley to search for wildlife. They spot a herd of bison passing through the valley. What a wonderful day in Yellowstone National Park!

YELLOWSTONE NATIONAL PARK

Yellowstone National Park is the oldest and one of the most popular national parks in the United States. Most of the park is in northwestern Wyoming. It also spills into southern Montana and eastern Idaho.

Yellowstone covers 3,472 square miles (8,991 square kilometers) of mountains, prairies, and canyons. The park is home to many animals that can be seen from the Grand Loop Road. Yellowstone rests on top of a **volcano**. This is the reason for the park's many **geysers** and hot springs. Old Faithful is the park's most famous geyser. It **erupts** around 20 times every day!

MONTANA

GRAND LOOP ROAD

OLD FAITHFUL

IDAHO

WYOMING

N
W+E
S

■ = YELLOWSTONE NATIONAL PARK

OLD FAITHFUL

SMELLY SITES

Many of Yellowstone's features give off a rotten egg smell. This odor is caused by a gas called hydrogen sulfide.

THE LAND

ABYSS POOL HOT SPRING

HOT TOPIC

The last major volcanic eruption in Yellowstone was around 640,000 years ago.

Yellowstone began forming millions of years ago. Movement of Earth's **tectonic plates** thinned the planet's **crust**. The thin crust meant **magma** was closer to the surface. This led to volcanic eruptions in the area. After each of these events, the land collapsed and formed a **caldera**.

Yellowstone's volcanic activity has shaped much of the park today. It created the famous hot springs and geysers, as well as the park's mountains and **plateaus**. Every year, Yellowstone has hundreds of small earthquakes. These are caused by movements of the tectonic plates.

HOW GEYSERS ERUPT

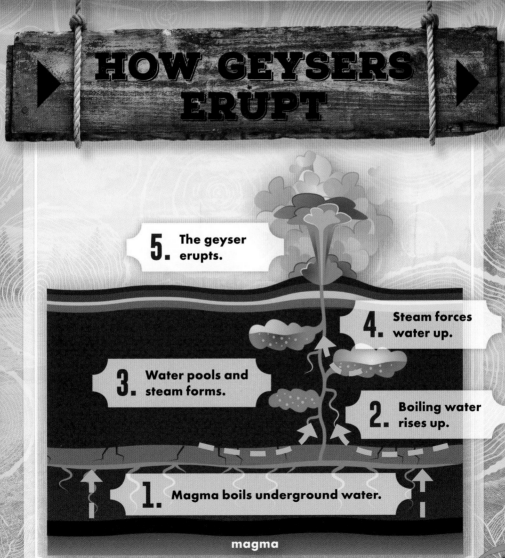

5. The geyser erupts.

4. Steam forces water up.

3. Water pools and steam forms.

2. Boiling water rises up.

1. Magma boils underground water.

magma

Yellowstone is full of mountains. In the east, the Absaroka Range is home to the park's highest point, Eagle Peak. The Gallatin Range is in the northwest. Both ranges are part of the Rocky Mountains. The park also has many lakes and rivers. Yellowstone Lake lies in the center of the park. The Yellowstone River flows north through the park. It creates a two-part waterfall as it flows through the Grand Canyon of the Yellowstone.

ABSAROKA RANGE

YELLOWSTONE LAKE

AVERAGE TEMPERATURES

JANUARY
- ▲ HIGH: 29°F (-2°C)
- ▼ LOW: 10°F (-12°C)

APRIL
- ▲ HIGH: 49°F (9°C)
- ▼ LOW: 26°F (-3°C)

JULY
- ▲ HIGH: 80°F 27°C)
- ▼ LOW: 47°F (8°C)

OCTOBER
- ▲ HIGH: 56°F (13°C)
- ▼ LOW: 29°F (-2°C)

°F = degrees Fahrenheit   °C = degrees Celsius

Yellowstone's climate varies by **elevation**. Higher areas are colder and receive more snow in the winter. Temperatures are often mild in the summer, though nights can be cold in higher parts of the park.

PLANTS AND WILDLIFE

Most of Yellowstone is covered in forests. Lodgepole pines are the most common tree in the park. Whitebark pines are typical in higher areas, and Douglas firs are common in lower parts of Yellowstone. Songbirds such as chickadees make homes in Yellowstone's trees. Northern flickers peck into the trees in search of food. Bald eagles soar overhead.

The forests of Yellowstone are home to large animals such as moose. Wolves are also common throughout the park. They often eat elk and mule deer. Foxes and coyotes are also found in the area. They often hunt jackrabbits and other small mammals.

WHITEBARK PINE

MOUNTAIN CHICKADEE

MOOSE

GRAY WOLF

JACKRABBIT

BALD EAGLE

Life Span: up to 30 years
Status: least concern

bald eagle range = ■

LEAST CONCERN	NEAR THREATENED	VULNERABLE	ENDANGERED	CRITICALLY ENDANGERED	EXTINCT IN THE WILD	EXTINCT

AMERICAN BISON

Life Span: up to 20 years
Status: near threatened

American bison range = ■

LEAST CONCERN	NEAR THREATENED	VULNERABLE	ENDANGERED	CRITICALLY ENDANGERED	EXTINCT IN THE WILD	EXTINCT

▲

Cottonwood and willow trees line the park's streams. The most common native fish in the park's waters is the Yellowstone cutthroat trout. These are often eaten by black bears, grizzly bears, and river otters. There are groups of American white pelicans on Yellowstone Lake in the summer. American dippers eat insects out of streams. Western tiger salamanders are common in fishless waters.

Many wildflowers bloom in Yellowstone's prairies. Cinquefoils and Indian paintbrushes are common in the Hayden and Lamar Valleys. Bison and pronghorn also roam these areas. Prairie rattlesnakes slither among the flowers and grasses in northern Yellowstone.

INDIAN PAINTBRUSHES

AMERICAN DIPPER

LOOKING SHARP

Obsidian was often shaped into tools, spear tips, and arrowheads. Pieces of this volcanic glass from Yellowstone have been found across North America.

OBSIDIAN

People have been in Yellowstone for at least 11,000 years. The earliest visitors likely hunted in the area during the summer. Early Native Americans also gathered plants and searched for **obsidian**.

CASTLE GEYSER

Yellowstone's geysers and hot springs had spiritual meaning for some Native Americans. People also came to the area to trade. As recently as the 1800s, around ten tribes still lived near Yellowstone Lake. Among these tribes were the Bannock, Blackfeet, Crow, Flathead, Nez Percé, and Shoshone.

The first white visitors to Yellowstone arrived in the 1700s. These fur trappers traded with Native Americans in the area. In 1806, the Lewis and Clark **Expedition** passed near the area. A member of this group, John Colter, returned in 1807.

Word of Colter's journey spread. More trappers and explorers began visiting the area in the 1820s. The first map of the region was made in 1836. In the 1860s and 1870s, the government sent more expeditions to explore the area. These trips built support for creating a national park at Yellowstone.

PAINTING BY THOMAS MORAN

ART MATTERS

Artists helped draw attention to making Yellowstone a national park. Paintings by Thomas Moran and photographs from William Henry Jackson showed others Yellowstone's beauty.

LOWER FALLS OF THE YELLOWSTONE RIVER

Much of the support for a national park came from railroad companies. They wanted to build railways across the country. **Tourism** from national parks would help increase interest in their trains. By 1872, President Ulysses S. Grant signed the bill creating Yellowstone National Park.

PRESIDENT
ULYSSES S. GRANT

The National Park Service was created in 1916. They took over responsibility for Yellowstone from the Army soon after.

MAMMOTH
HOT SPRINGS HOTEL & CABINS

The Northern Pacific Railroad reached the area in the early 1880s. A hotel was built around the same time at Mammoth Hot Springs. In the mid-1880s, the United States Army began overseeing Yellowstone. They improved the park's roads and buildings. They also put an end to animal **poaching**. Today, Yellowstone welcomes around 4 million visitors to the park each year.

VISITING YELLOWSTONE NATIONAL PARK

Cars were first allowed in Yellowstone in 1915. Today, they are the most common way for visitors to see the park. Many visitors drive on park roads to see Old Faithful, Grand Prismatic Spring, and other famous attractions.

SNOWCOACH

CROSS-COUNTRY SKIING

BOILING RIVER

Visitors can swim in Yellowstone's Boiling River! Here, water from hot springs mixes with cool water from the Gardner River.

TOP SITES

GRAND CANYON OF THE YELLOWSTONE

GRAND PRISMATIC SPRING

MAMMOTH HOT SPRINGS

OLD FAITHFUL

Yellowstone's more than 900 miles (1,448 kilometers) of trails are perfect for hiking. Fishing and boating are also popular in the park. Most of Yellowstone's roads are closed to cars in the winter. Snowmobiles and **snowcoaches** are used instead. Yellowstone is a favorite place to snowshoe and cross-country ski.

PROTECTING THE PARK

Millions of people visit Yellowstone each year. The number of visitors can cause problems in the park. It increases **erosion** and can harm plant and animal **habitats**. Tourists must follow directions on signs and stay on marked paths and boardwalks. This helps protect plants and animals in the park. It also protects visitors from unsafe areas of the park.

Another important way that visitors can protect Yellowstone is to help keep animals wild. Visitors should not approach or feed wildlife. They should keep away from animals while walking or hiking. If an animal is near their car, they should stay inside and keep the windows closed.

MOURNING GLORY

Littering has changed Yellowstone's hot springs. Morning Glory Pool used to be blue in color. Trash thrown in the pool lowered its temperature, which caused its colors to change.

Yellowstone is also threatened by **climate change**. Warming temperatures are changing the park's normal seasonal patterns. Less snowfall and drier summers are becoming more common. This makes it harder for plants and animals to survive. It also increases the risk of wildfires.

WILDFIRE DAMAGE

The park is working to protect Yellowstone from the effects of climate change. Some buildings use **solar power** to lower fuel use. The park is also working to waste less water. Visitors can help, too. They can drive electric cars when they visit the park. They can put out campfires to lower the risk of wildfires. If everyone does their part, the wonders of Yellowstone will remain for the future!

GRAND PRISMATIC SPRING

YELLOWSTONE NATIONAL PARK FACTS

Area: **3,472** square miles
(8,991 square kilometers)

Annual Visitors:
4.9 million visitors in 2021

Area Rank: **8**TH
largest park

Population Rank: **3**RD
most visited park in 2021

Date Established:
March 1, 1872

Highest point: Eagle Peak;
11,358 feet (3,462 meters)

TIMELINE

11,000
YEARS AGO

The first Native American
peoples visit the
Yellowstone area

1700s

White fur trappers
arrive and trade with
Native Americans

FOOD WEB

GRAY WOLF

ELK

BISON

ASPEN BARK

GRASSES AND SEDGES

1807

John Colter visits Yellowstone after exploring with Lewis and Clark

1915

Personal cars are first allowed in Yellowstone

1872

Yellowstone becomes the world's first national park

GLOSSARY

caldera—a large crater formed by a volcano

climate change—a human-caused change in Earth's weather due to warming temperatures

crust—the outer layer of Earth's surface

elevation—height above sea level

erosion—the process through which rocks are worn away by wind, water, or ice

erupts—suddenly lets out steam, water, or other materials

expedition—a journey with a purpose, such as to explore an area

geysers—springs that shoot out jets of hot water or steam

habitats—natural homes of plants and animals

hot springs—places where hot water flows out of the ground

magma—melted rock within the earth

obsidian—a hard, dark rock that looks like glass

plateaus—areas of flat, raised land

poaching—illegally hunting or fishing

snowcoaches—large vehicles that have big tires or tracks for traveling through snow

solar power—power from the sun

tectonic plates—large pieces of the earth's crust

terraces—series of flat, level areas on a slope

tourism—the business of people traveling to visit other places

volcano—a hole in the earth that erupts hot ash, gas, or melted rock called lava

TO LEARN MORE

AT THE LIBRARY

Leaf, Christina. *Wyoming*. Minneapolis, Minn.: Bellwether Media, 2022.

McCarthy, Cecilia Pinto. *Yellowstone National Park*. Minneapolis, Minn.: Abdo Publishing, 2017.

Payne, Stefanie. *National Parks: Discover All 62 Parks of the United States*. New York, N.Y.: DK Publishing, 2020.

ON THE WEB

FACTSURFER

Factsurfer.com gives you a safe, fun way to find more information.

1. Go to www.factsurfer.com.

2. Enter "Yellowstone National Park" into the search box and click ￼.

3. Select your book cover to see a list of related content.

INDEX

The images in this book are reproduced through the courtesy of: Mia2you, cover; RaksyBH, p. 3; Filip Fuxa, p. 5 (Grand Canyon of the Yellowstone), 25 (Morning Glory Pool); GJ-NYC, pp. 4-5; Susanne Pommer, pp. 6-7; Lynn Yeh, p. 8; Julie Lubick, p. 10 (Absaroka Range); Virrage Images, p. 10 (Yellowstone Lake); Kris Wiktor, p. 11; Kjetil Kolbjornsrud, p. 12 (gray wolf); Sue Smith, p. 12 (whitebark pine); My Generations Art, p. 12 (mountain chickadee); Petr Simon, p. 12 (moose); Tom Reichner, pp. 12 (jackrabbit), 14; FloridaStock, p. 13; Timothy Epp, p. 15 (indian paintbrushes); Carrie Olson, p. 15 (American dipper); NPS Photo/ Alamy, pp. 16 (obsidian), 22 (cross-country skiing); Harry Beugelink, pp. 16-17; Thomas Moran/ Wikipedia, p. 18 (painting by Thomas Moran); Carolina Wild Productions, pp. 18-19; Everett Collection, p. 20 (President Ulysses S. Grant); Cheri Alguire, p. 20; Gabbro/ Alamy, p. 21; Adam Reck, p. 22 (snowcoach); Jason Patrick Ross, p. 23 (Grand Canyon of the Yellowstone); Lorcel, p. 23 (Grand Prismatic Spring); Randy Runtsch, p. 23 (Old Faithful); mark lee/ Alamy, p. 24; melissamn, pp. 24-25; Louise Heusinkveld/ Alamy, p. 26 (wildfire damage); Jessica Towns, pp. 26-27; Vaclav Sebek, pp. 28-29, 30-31, 32; Oomka, p. 28 (11,000 years ago); North Wind Picture Archive/ Alamy, p. 28 (1700s); Miguel Angel Muñoz Pellicer/ Alamy, p. 29 (1807); Chase Clausen, p. 29 (1872); Chronicle/ Alamy, p. 29 (1915); Vlada Cech, p 29 (gray wolf); Cornelius Doppes, p. 29 (elk); Grey Mountain Photo, p. 29 (bison); Ryan DeBerardinis, p. 29 (aspen bark); USFWS Mountain-Prairie/ Wikipedia, p. 29 (grasses and sedges); Agami Photo Agency, p. 31.